Capturing Meaning

The Essence of Being Human

haikus by

Jerrell J. Ferguson

Copyright © 2022 by Jerrell J. Ferguson

All rights reserved. No part of this book may be reproduced in any form, stored in any retrieval system, or transmitted in any form by any means, electronic, mechanical, photocopy, recording, or otherwise except for use of brief quotations in a review.

ISBN: 978-1-951713-38-6 (ebook)
ISBN: 978-1-951713-37-9 (hardcover)
ISBN: 978-1-951713-36-2 (paperback)

Various Illustrations: © 2022 by Jana Leigh, used with permission
Haiku on Back Cover: © 2021 by Susan Ferguson, used with permission
Interior and Cover Design: Laura Acton

Three Fates Publishing

Contents

Preface	i
Physical wounds heal	1
A little boy died	2
For what do I hope	3
Death for the unwise	4
Bile personified	5
Eager for gentle strokes	6
Gypsy girl Jana	7
Lovely Beverly	8
They oughta be dead	9
Honor to the house	10
Do not marry her	11
Gets the devil out of them	12
Thinks outside the box	13
Smilin' sunshine Sue	14
Traits of real worth	15
Hail the grand new day	16
Guilty I lived it	17
Said the existentialist	18
Needs a bright lodestar	19
Comparatively	20
Enemies fight wars	21
Empty is empty	22
Soldiers die in war	23
The last act of love	24
Years past someone said	25
Unrequited love	26
Ignores the mind	27
Dulling our senses	28
Basics for a strong house	29
Remember them well	30
So say the wordsmiths	31
Where are you Haiku	32
My friend follow through	33
Excuse my lost muse	34
Using the word love	35
Is not simply a question	36
From grief's tight embrace	37

Beauty you don't know	38
As two hearts entwine	39
The cool taste of rain	40
From ashes of my loss	41
What we are will pass	42
Death took him away	43
For one who needs it	44
Blood ran in rivers	45
Living off of you	46
How shadowed are we	47
We did it for us	48
Arizona pinks and blues	49
Philosophy tries	50
In the still of the night	51
Beautiful dreamer	52
Am I my brother's keeper	53
Beware of humans	54
Trust but verify	55
Zip a dee doo dah	56
Never the same people	57
Inflation data	58
Clueless classless republic	59
Speaking of material	60
Buy low and sell high	61
Kisses will wake you	62
Be not first to try	63
Huge flower arrays	64
Cruising through the universe	65
Princess unaware	66
You may regret it	67
He heard the ocean	68
Lighting lovers' lane	69
Warming to a bright new day	70
This place we call our home	71
Hail the morning sun	72
Bringing love and joy	73
Land of liberty	74
Bring smiles back to me	75
Dance O graceful art	76
The greatest life gift	77
Finding the beauty	78
Fickle - life has shown	79

O Brave new morning	80
We will never know	81
No need for much talk	82
Go yell scream and shout	83
Entwined in mystery	84
They touch - kiss	85
Who will come to help	86
Where an angel should be	87
If we are to die	88
Wedded bliss soon ends	89
A loss I cannot replace	90
A colorful start	91
People who have left	92
Fit to be tied	93
Playing with words	94
The most quiet sounds	95
If I do not care	96
It is ironic	97
True uncertainty	98
Toss away your assumptions	99
To know you must ask	100
Let your soul be free	101
I have lost myself	102
It is never out of style	103
During World War Two	104
It will work if you	105
Where is Kyle's Haiku	106
American boys	107
Fear of darkness dies	108
Daily if you can	109
Humans like to fight	110
To know what evil is	111
Whose ambitions remain	112
Who's going to Hell	113
He has little twists	114
Good advice - bad ears	115
Beautiful Black Hills	116
The dawn of the day	117
Sad what I will miss	118
Greet me so gently	119
I'll be back my dear	120
Eyes tell your story	121

The loveliest ever seen	122
Half angel half beast	123
I try hard to cope	124
Because of our mortal crust	125
Time to remember	126
Life is a silhouette	127
Not too young to die	128
Our love was born dead	129
So some people pray	130
In our long journey	131
Tears roll from your eyes	132
One life and one love	133
Rejuxtapositioning	134
Could tear me away	135
What choices have we	136
They will regret it	137
What can they be worth	138
Unless it comes to driving	139
Spend time in nowhere	140
Sex without true love	141
Learning female wiles	142
He left home all knew his name	143
Raw emotion lasts	144
Perfect human hands	145
Gentle on my mind	146
So ambiguous	147
If you want to speak	148
Subtly hide should nots	149
Where are you going	150
Check up on your tools	151
Live your dream each day	152
About the Author	153

Capturing Meaning

The Essence of Being Human

Preface

A haiku is said to be a three-line poem with a syllable count as follows:

>Five in the first line
>Seven in the second line
>Five in the third line

This is the form of the haiku and it is correct. What does it say? You could write lines like that all night and never actually write a haiku. The soul of the haiku is a concise nature picture, a concise insight, a concise observation, and a concise dream or imagined event. Something beautifully worded eliciting reactions in the reader.

Using Japanese, a language having several short words with two to four syllables, it becomes easier to follow those rules. English is quite different so writing requires fewer syllables.

Upon reviewing my haikus, I discovered useless words inserted solely to meet the syllabic count. I decided to eliminate them and found they read much better, more like Basho's haikus, without the filler words. Removing one 'of', one 'that', or one 'the', made a significant difference.

I always write in the correct form then amend the poem as needed to meet the primary requisite of a good haiku, making lines one and three shorter than line two.

Samuel T. Coleridge wrote, "Poetry is the best words in the best order." I try.

Physical wounds heal
New love can heal your heartache
Not wounds to the soul

A little boy died
What could he have been
We will never know

If only sorrow
Awaits tomorrow
For what do I hope

Ice caps cold snowy
Gorgeous mountains beckoning
Death for the unwise

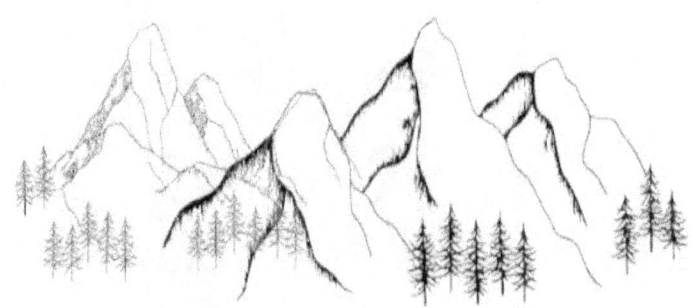

Hate hate more hate
Blots on the beauty of life
Bile personified

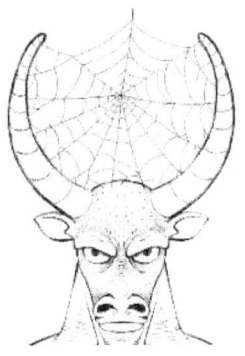

A bit of tissue
Eager for gentle strokes
People need contact

Gypsy girl Jana
Dancing across the country
In her Janbulance

Lovely Beverly
Sweeter than the morning dew
Her smile wakes dawn

Novelist Laura
Whumps her heroes pretty bad
They oughta be dead

Honor to the house
Home where you were born
Those who love you

Young man if your love
Does not love her own mother
Do not marry her

Brad a details man
Gets the devil out of them
From start to finish

Jeff the inventive
Does not ask why but why not
Thinks outside the box

Smilin' sunshine Sue
Cooks and teaches Biology
They are much alike

Nancy's books and plants
Intellect and down to earth
Traits of real worth

Saguaro cacti
As far as the eye can see
Hail the grand new day

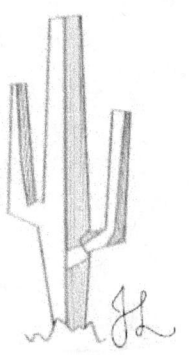

I reviewed my life
Brought in my own verdict
Guilty I lived it

I yam that I yam
Said the existentialist
At least I think so

Steve with potential
Still searching for who he is
Needs a bright lodestar

Brenton the thinker
Considers differences
Comparatively

Enemies fight wars
War is on the people
Men women and kids

Nothing to pray for
No where to go on this earth
Empty is empty

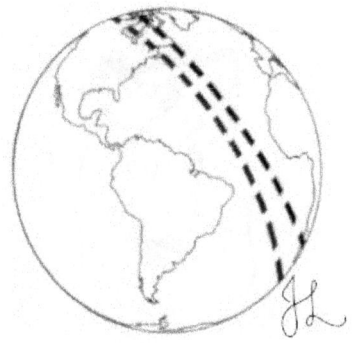

Soldiers die in war
Others also pay a price
Raped maimed or murdered

The last act of love
Give all that you have
To those who love you

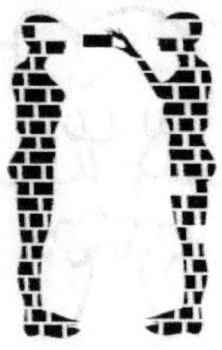

Years past someone said
All we have to fear is fear
It is true today

Heartaches to hatred
Short of a New York minute
Unrequited love

Whoever said
Beauty is only skin deep
Ignores the mind

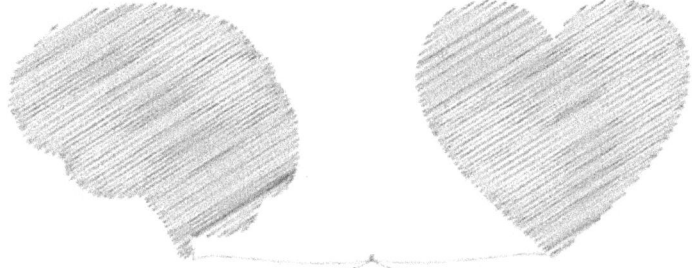

Fatigue pain and stress
Daily dose of routine
Dulling our senses

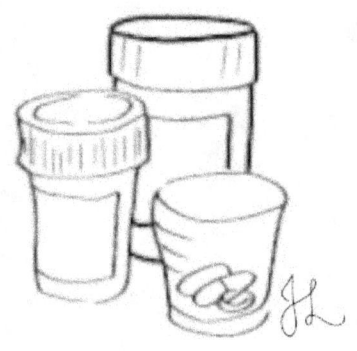

Wood - stone - glass pane
Basics for a strong house
Floors - walls - windows

Whatever you do
Do not forget the good times
Remember them well

It must be written
Else it will fade away
So say the wordsmiths

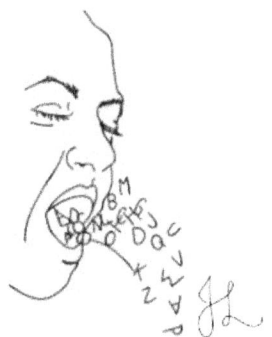

Where are you Haiku
You were written in my head
Now lost in my mind

My friend follow through
Got up and said, 'I am through'
So I can't finish

No Haiku for you
Nor any Poetry from me
Excuse my lost muse

Using the word love
What in the world does it mean
What you say it means

To exist or not
Is not simply a question
But a conclusion

From grief's tight embrace
Streams of tears streak past time
Into a sea of love

Beauty you don't know
You display a special glow
Dark you cannot do

As two hearts entwine
In space and time life begins
When two become one

The cool taste of rain
Impressions of loveliness
Sweet clean images

A little bird wings
From the ashes of my loss
Love will never die

What we are will pass
So let us be what we are
For the time we have

Brother Larry Dean
I do not know where he is
Death took him away

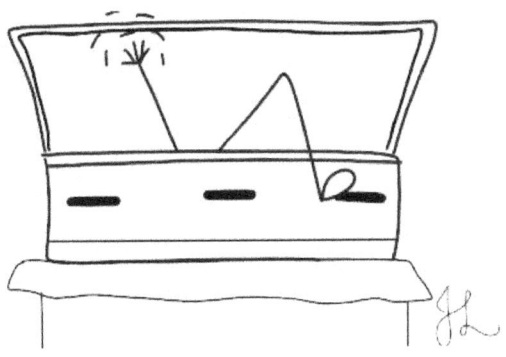

Try each day you live
To do at least one good deed
For one who needs it

Blood ran in rivers
You were lucky if not dead
But then maybe not

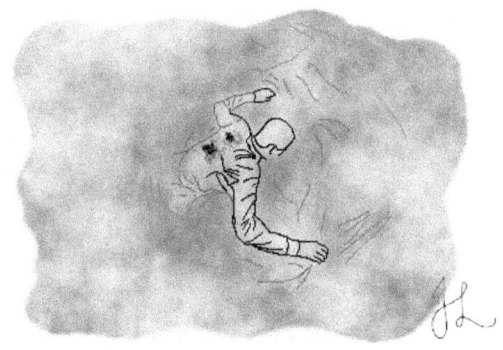

You have a fetus
A human inside of you
Living off of you

Our sins cast shadows
Older sins longer shadows
How shadowed are we

We did it for us
Skimping working together
A true family

Beautiful sunsets
Arizona pinks and blues
Light the dusky sky

Philosophy tries
To find higher ideals
That fit human minds

Capturing Meaning 51

In the still of the night
Old embarrassments recur
From nowhere it seems

Beautiful dreamer
Ignoring reality
May cost you dearly

Brother Larry Dean
Am I my brother's keeper
But I was not there

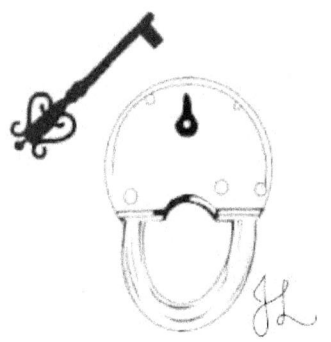

Beware of humans
They cheat and prevaricate
In multiple ways

If it's important
And you must really know
Trust but verify

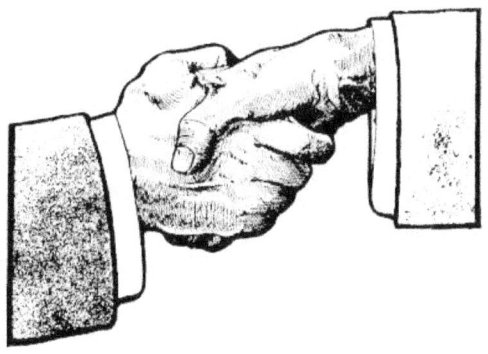

Zip a dee doo dah
It is a wonderful day
Time to die happy

Poor live with us
Never the same people
It's true of the rich

Compare rich to poor
A statistic nothing more
Inflation data

Good old U.S. of A.
Clueless classless republic
Maybe, maybe not

What happens to me
Speaking of material
Will not matter much

Buy low and sell high
A stock pickers cry so why
Do people buy high

Beautiful dreamer
Asleep in an ancient song
Kisses will wake you

Be not first to try
Whatever is new and great
And be not too late

This is May today
Thirty-one days of May
Huge flower arrays

Bev and I sit here
Cruising through the universe
On our comfy chairs

Princess unaware
Asleep in an ancient song
A prince will wake you

Do not be too late
To meet a brand new blind date
You may regret it

He heard the ocean
Eagerly waiting to kiss
Edges of the shore

She saw moonbeams
Zip across the midnight sky
Lighting lovers' lane

He saw the sun rise
Warming to a bright new day
With rose pinks and gray

Earth spins around the sun
This place we call our home
Meets all of our needs

Hail the morning sun
Beautiful to all eyes
Welcome the warm day

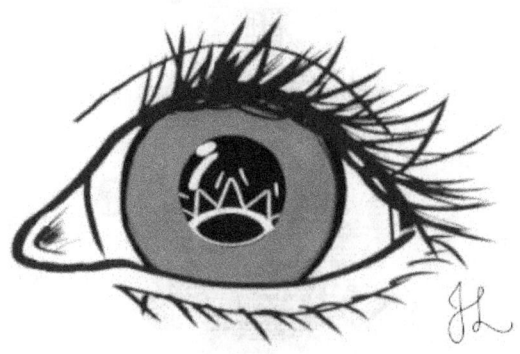

She was beautiful
Warm as a summertime day
Bringing love and joy

O' America
God bestows his grace on thee
Land of liberty

Bring smiles back to me
Bring back dawn's new glow to me
Keep her near to me

Dance O graceful art
Upright expression of a
Recumbent desire

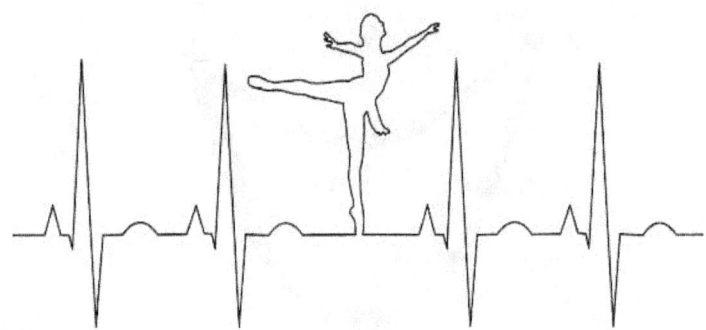

Ah refreshing rain
Pours from the sky again and again
The greatest life gift

Finding the beauty
In all I feel hear or see
Makes a better me

Oh reality
A measure of all that's known
Fickle - life has shown

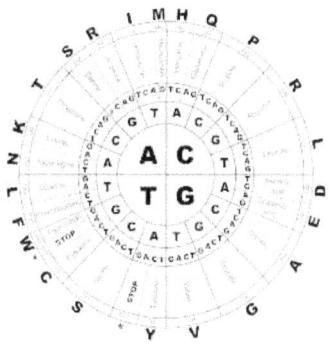

O Brave new morning
What have you to say today
Clear, I heard it say

How it happened
Love made for the two of us
We will never know

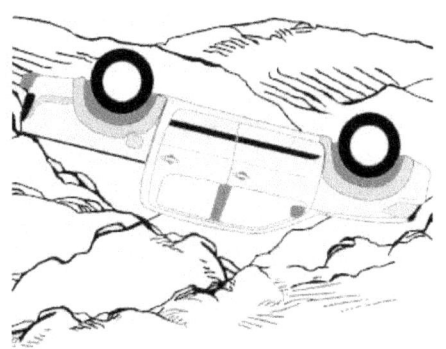

No need for much talk
A loving gaze will suffice
Or a simple touch

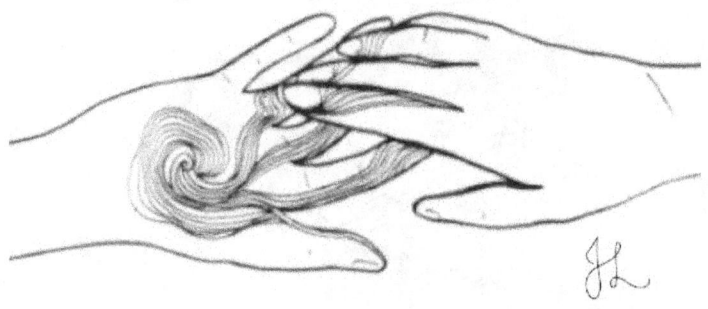

Go yell scream and shout
Out pain! Out pain! Get out! Out!
The cost of love lost

Two lovers you see
Entwined in mystery
However did they meet

They touch - kiss
Displaying grace
Love on each face

Who will come to help
When the storm lightning or gale
Turns you into dust

Beautiful to see
Heaven sent and back again
Where an angel should be

If we are to die
Would the last thought be
Where we are going?

Wedded bliss soon ends
Work and bills are piling up
Children start to grow

So much love from her
A loss I cannot replace
Dreams are gone

Beautiful sunrise
Pink interspersed with blue
A colorful start

People who have left
Leave you wondering why
One reason… they die

You are in love now
Looking for that lover's knot
Fit to be tied

Playing with words
Those wonderful tools of thought
Giving out great joy

In a green forest
Amid the beauty I hear
The most quiet sounds

If I do not care
What you do or where you go
You will never know

It is ironic
Laugh at society and
Your self to improve

We begin to cope
With ignorance as we see
True uncertainty

Understand your world
Toss away your assumptions
Question openly

To know you must ask
It was Socrates prime task
He paid with his life

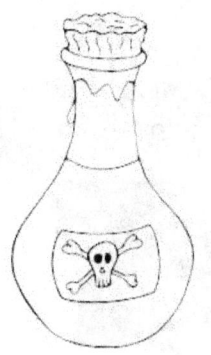

Let your soul be free
Disconnect from the mundane
Go laugh in the rain

I have lost myself
Trapped in her deep deep love
I will never leave

When it comes to love
It is never out of style
High fashion or nude

Helping the effort
Mr. Wheeler capped tires
During World War Two

It will work if you
Bask in sun and gaze at moon
But not the reverse

106 *Jerrell J. Ferguson*

Looking through a proof
Mom noted an omission
Where is Kyle's Haiku

American boys
Red white and blue to the core
Could you ask for more

Fear of darkness dies
If death darkens your bright skies
It leaves you too cold

Try to do good deeds
For one who has real needs
Daily if you can

Humans like to fight
Don't matter if war is hell
If you live to tell

To know what evil is
You need to know good from sin
Culture rules again

Whose ambitions remain
Within reasonable bounds
To achieve success

Who's going to Hell
It may be too hard to tell
So - go flip a coin

Want to read a poet
Then try Edgar Alan Poe
He has little twists

Good advice - bad ears
Too late as our old age nears
To heed old wise words

I left my troubles
In the clean breath of nature
Beautiful Black Hills

The dawn of the day
In its own special way shows
Colors bright and gay

Valentine's Day
No one to hug or to kiss
Sad what I will miss

Brown hair and brown eyes
The full bloom of sweet red lips
Greet me so gently

I'll be back my dear
We'll be as one forever
Longer if we can

Eyes tell your story
One as old as love itself
That will never change

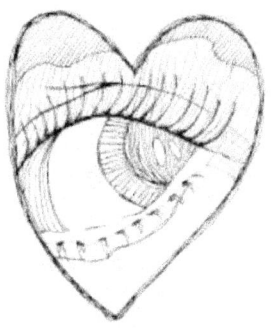

Cheerful happy teen
The loveliest ever seen
Brightens every day

Half angel half beast
Dreamy watcher of the stars
Do not fret your fate

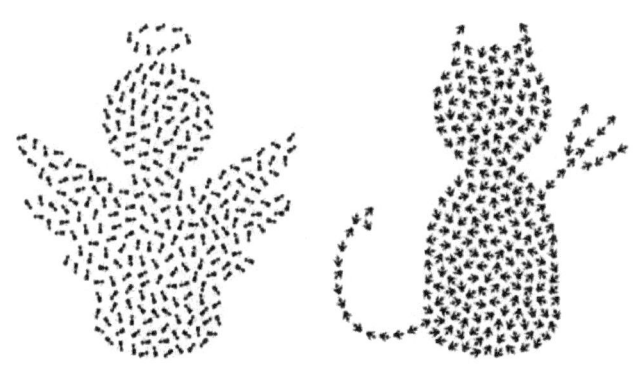

My load is heavy
Where is my comfort and hope
I try hard to cope

We will turn to dust
Because of our mortal crust
Learn to live with it

Time to remember
Our loved ones too early gone
Our joy of past years

Life is a silhouette
Death the profound end of life
Love is for young hearts

Not too young to die
Then we must always ask 'Why?'
We ask 'What?' if old

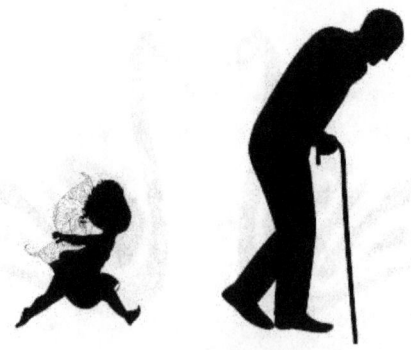

Our love was born dead
None of the right words were said
Stuck inside my head

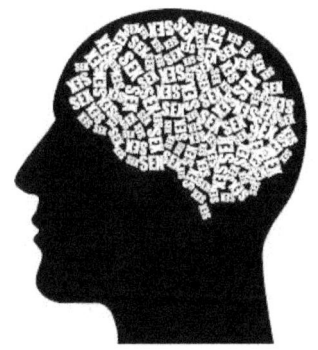

God is everywhere
All the time and all knowing
So some people pray

I think we will come
To a dark confusing time
In our long journey

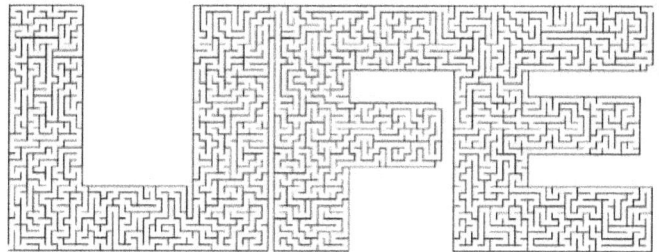

Looking back you feel
Emotions that were so strong
Tears roll from your eyes

One life and one love
Were not destiny for me
Two and maybe three

Ever constant change
Rejuxtapositioning
We just call it time

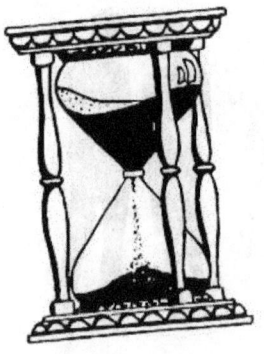

Bed is nice and warm
Only the duty of day
Could tear me away

What choices have we
Without subjective freedom
None that I can see

The human destroyers
Pollute ruin and ravage earth
They will regret it

What can they be worth
Things of value to hold dear
Or to toss away

Gambling is a vice
Unless it comes to driving
What are traffics odds

Spend time in nowhere
You could go stark raving mad
Without stimuli

Sex without true love
Is like playing racket ball
Only exercise

Learning female wiles
May take more than one lifetime
And many trials

Unknown Soldier boy
He left home all knew his name
No one knows it now

Killed by a fast car
Family kept it from me
Raw emotion lasts

Perfect human hands
A perfect match for our brain
Perfect loves hold hands

The best college days
Events easy to recall
Gentle on my mind

God is great and good
She may be likelihood
So ambiguous

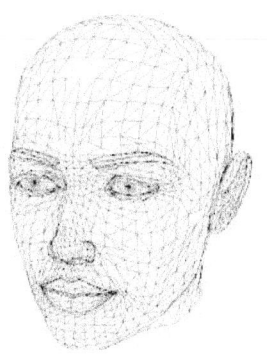

If you want to speak
Really communicate
Arrange your best words

Show us that you care
Do it with joy and with flair
Subtly hide should nots

Where are you going
What happens when you get there
You set a new goal

What is your new aim
Is it even reachable
Check up on your tools

Live your dream each day
Be joyful happy and dance
Give romance a chance

I hope you found a favorite or two.

About the Author

Jerrell wrote his first poem at ten and has composed them consistently throughout his life. An English Literature teacher planted the seed that ideas and feelings could be succinctly yet broadly and powerfully expressed in a few words.

His style is influenced by quotes from Samuel Taylor Coleridge, 'Poetry is the best words in the best order,' and Shakespeare, 'brevity is the soul of wit.'

He holds a graduate degree in Psychology, and worked with special needs children as a school psychologist for several years before teaching college for over three decades.

Jerrell's poems about what it means to be human are inspired by insights gained from a desire to comprehend the world we live in, life experiences, family, friends, and a love of creating word patterns.

www.ingramcontent.com/pod-product-compliance
Lightning Source LLC
Chambersburg PA
CBHW061948070426
42450CB00007BA/1086